J. Mason Brewer

Negro Folklorist

BY JAMES W. BYRD
East Texas State University

STECK-VAUGHN COMPANY AUSTIN, TEXAS

A native of Alabama, James W. Byrd earned his B.A. degree there at Troy State College. His M.A. and Ph.D. degrees were awarded by George Peabody College, where his dissertation was entitled "White Character Portrayal by Negro Novelists, 1900-1950." He has published articles on Negro literature, Negro folklorist Zora Neale Hurston, and general folklore of the Southwest. He was president of the Texas Folklore Society in 1965. He is a regular book reviewer for the Greenville *Herald Banner*, *Tennessee Folklore Bulletin*, and *Phylon Quarterly*. James W. Byrd is now professor of English at East Texas State University in Commerce, where part of the research on J. Mason Brewer was done with the help of a faculty research grant.

Library of Congress Catalog Card Number 67-25230

J. Mason Brewer

Negro Folklorist

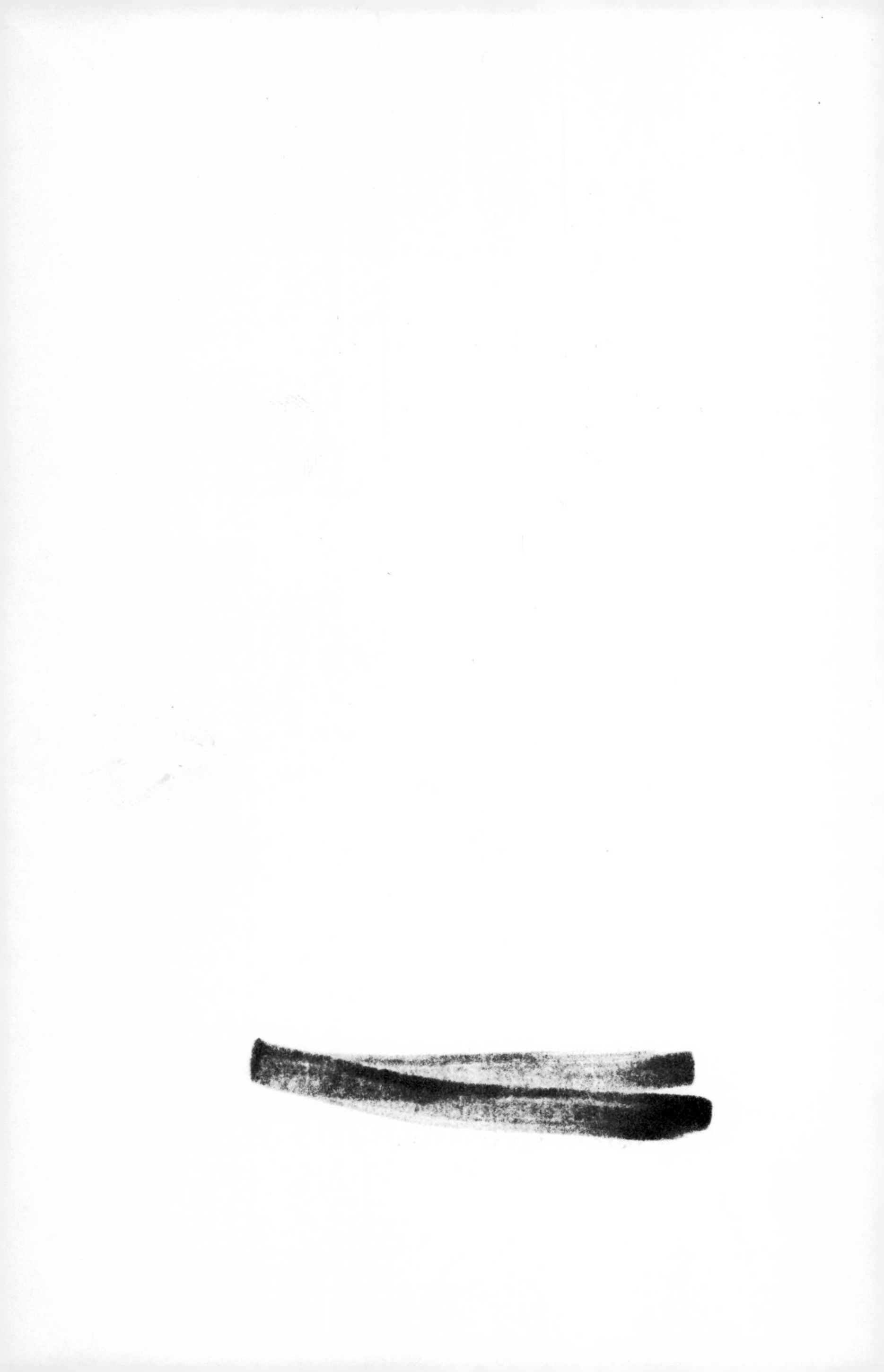

J. Mason Brewer
Negro Folklorist

"THE STATE'S ONE NEGRO writer of importance," wrote George Fuermann about fellow-Texan J. Mason Brewer in *Reluctant Empire,* and historian W. Eugene Hollon echoed him in *The Southwest: Old and New.* Brewer, a vigorous septuagenarian, is the most distinguished living Negro folklorist; that is, he is a folklorist, he is a Negro, and he collects and publishes the folklore of the Negro—preacher tales, trickster tales, anecdotes, proverbs, and ghost stories. A prolific writer, he also produces poems, essays, reviews, and anthologies. His work received the praise of his most learned contemporaries, exemplified by the "Texas Triumvirate of Letters"—J. Frank Dobie, Roy Bedichek, and Walter Prescott Webb. Frank H. Wardlaw was a friend and benefactor. Scholars of other sections of the world interested in the development of Southwestern literature—Stith Thompson, Arthur Palmer Hudson, Archer Taylor, and John Jacob Niles—welcomed his participation in national folklore discussions and publications. He was associated with John A. and Alan Lomax in the Folklore Institute at Indiana University. He has well represented the Negro—past and present—as a researcher, writer, and speaker.

John Mason Brewer was born in Goliad, Texas, near Bahia Mission, on March 24, 1896. There were four sisters and one brother in the literary-minded family. Dr. Stella Brewer Brookes, chairman of the English Department at Clark College in Atlanta, a published authority on Joel Chandler Harris as folklorist, credits her brother with first stimulating her interest in folklore. The three other sisters—Marguerite, Gladys, and Jewell—joined school faculties in Houston and Austin. Claude, Brewer's only brother, is an interior decorator in Austin.

The four out of five teachers among the children were obviously influenced by the mother, Minnie T. Brewer, who taught fifty years in the public schools of Texas. On her side of the family, "Aunt" Eliza Clomn lived in Fannin, Texas, owning land adjoining the battleground where General James W. Fannin and his men were slaughtered by the Mexican troops in the Texas War for Independence. On visits, young Mason picked up old bullets probably fired into Fannin's Brigade. Eager for more history and spurred by the ever-present family folktales, the lad was not satisfied just to read the paperbacks about Jesse James, Nick Carter, and Buffalo Bill.

His father, as well as his mother, influenced him. J. H. Brewer led a varied life with occupations determined by the Texas of his time—wagoner, mail carrier, postmaster, grocer, and barber—but he was not unsettled. His five children were born in homes he owned. He worked vigorously until he was ninety-two, when he died after falling from a step. Brewer is saturated with stories of the Old West told to him by his father, a drover who, in his young days, made trail drives to the Kansas railheads. J. H. Brewer was second trail boss on the Media Luna (Half-Moon) Ranch owned by Colonel D. R. Fant in Hidalgo County. He made several trips, as he told his son, to the Old Indian Territory during his trail-driving days. Like young Mason's two grandfathers, Joe Brewer and Pinckney Mitchell, who were wagoners hauling "notions" in the 1880's from Victoria to Goliad and Mission Refugio before the railroads came, the father delighted in telling Texas tales to a fascinated child. His mother guided him to Negro history books and the poems and stories of Paul Laurence Dunbar as soon as he could read. An avid listener became an avid reader as well. Later he became an avid writer.

"If we do not respect the past, the future will not respect us," Brewer wrote in 1963 in *Three Looks and Some Peeps*. He had arrived at this valuable conclusion by the time of the Texas

Centennial in 1936. In the preface to *The Negro in Texas History* he writes: "It would be impossible to tell the true story of Texas without including the various contributions made by the black race at frequent intervals to the building of this great empire."

He begins with "The Negro in Texas Exploration, 1528-1539" and reminds his reader that a Negro-Arab Moor, Estebanito (called Little Stephen), was with Cabeza de Vaca when he explored the territory from the Sabine River to the Rio Grande. In 1539, Little Stephen was employed by the Mexican Viceroy to lead a return expedition over the Cabeza de Vaca route. Though Little Stephen was killed on the expedition, many give him credit as being the discoverer of New Mexico.

In *The Negro in Texas History,* Brewer sketches in the era of slave trade in 1816-20 and tells the story of Kian Long, a slave girl of twelve in the Texas of 1820. The author gives her the title of Mother of Negro Texans, since she lived there before Stephen F. Austin established the first colony. She founded a family, and looking today at her descendants—appearing as substantial and educated citizens—one can believe in the advent of such another family as the Brewers in only a few generations on the frontier.

Young Mason Brewer attended the public schools of Austin and Fannin, and in 1913, at the age of seventeen, he was graduated. Four years later Wiley College in Marshall, Texas, awarded him a B.A. degree. He taught a year in Austin before joining the American Expeditionary Forces in 1918 after war was declared against Germany. He was stationed in France with the rank of corporal, where, because he knew French, Spanish, and Italian, his brigade officers called upon him to serve as interpreter. In 1919 he returned to the United States to become a teacher and principal in Fort Worth. In 1924 he left the profession briefly to work for an oil company in Denver, Colorado. There he began writing stories and verses for the company's trade journal and also for a monthly periodical, *The Negro American.* Two volumes of his verse had already been published. His desire to teach brought him back to the profession with a principalship in Shreveport and, in 1926, a professorship at Samuel Huston College in Austin. In the Texas capital city he met J. Frank Dobie, who was to be the biggest influence on his career as a writer.

In 1932, he crossed town to visit J. Frank Dobie with a shoe box full of Negro folktales. Dobie, then secretary-editor of the Texas Folklore Society, found them "genuine and delightful." Entitled "Juneteenth," they appeared in the Society's annual volume published that year. That was the beginning of a relationship of mutual advantage to Brewer and the Texas Folklore Society, whose members were to become familiar with his research at their annual conventions and in their annual publication of a volume of folklore.

The following year, 1933, Brewer first formally studied folklore under Professor Stith Thompson at the University of Indiana, where he received the Master of Arts degree. His final degree was an honorary one: the Doctor of Literature was bestowed on him by Paul Quinn College of Waco, Texas, in 1951.

After a year of teaching in Claflin College in Orangeburg, South Carolina, Brewer returned, in 1943, to the Austin college—now called Huston-Tillotson—as Chairman of the Department of English Language and Literature. He taught during the summers at Texas Southern University in Houston. Back in Austin, he pioneered a course called "The Negro in the Literature of the Southwest." He wanted his students, he said, to "realize the importance of their cultural heritage and the significance of their folklore as a living force." His students learned that one of the most original branches of American folklore is that of the Negro.

Since 1959 Brewer has been professor of English at Livingston College in Salisbury, North Carolina. He lives quietly in a home surrounded by many trees and flowering shrubs within walking distance of the college. His wife, Ruth Helen Brewer, is a kindergarten teacher. John Mason Brewer, Jr., a son by his first wife, serves with an adult education agency in Los Angeles, following, in the choice of profession, a Brewer family tradition.

Brewer's list of "firsts" is impressive. He became the first active Negro member of the Texas Folklore Society, publishing in four editions of its annual book of folklore. He is the only Negro author in the 1954 publication, *Texas Folk and Folklore,* which is a collection of articles on Texas folklore originally published in *Publications of the Texas Folklore Society.* Also in 1954 he was chosen as one of twenty-five best Texas authors by Theta Sigma Phi, Inc., national journalistic society. Subsequently he became the first Negro member of the Texas Institute of Letters. On the national level, he was the first Negro to serve on the council of the American Folklore Society, later becoming a vice-president. He was the first Negro to deliver a lecture series at leading Southwestern universities, including the Universities of Arizona, California, and Colorado. The General Education Board Fellowships and American Philosophical Society Fellowships provided opportunity for travel and research. Under these stimuli, Brewer left a record showing that he respects the past as well as the future of Negro lore and literature.

On the eve of the Texas Centennial in 1936, Brewer wrote in *The Negro in Texas History* of a folk custom caused by history:

> Since June 19, 1865, the Negroes in Texas have celebrated the date of their freedom with great enthusiasm. Programs, usually held in the open, are conducted, and great rejoicing is manifested on this day. The ex-slaves are always given special places on the program and special seats on the platforms. Songs, band music, the reading of the Emancipation Proclamation, and speaking share equally in the day's celebration. Always there is barbecue and watermelons to add to the pleasure of the occasion. The Negroes in Texas call this day's observance "Juneteenth" (p. 6).

In 1932, Brewer had used the name of this fading folk custom for his first significant publication. The collection of folktales called "Juneteenth" appeared in *Tone the Bell Easy*, tenth published collection of the Texas Folklore Society. Brewer had collected the tales for six or seven years. He heard them, he told Editor J. Frank Dobie, at country stores, on wagonloads of cotton, banks of fishing holes, rural schools and churches, and at Saturday night suppers and dances.

The antiquity of the forty traditional tales is indicated in the climax of one entitled "A Laugh That Meant Freedom." It concerns a bargain made by a slave with his master who never laughed. If he could be made to laugh, the master promised freedom for the joker.

> "Ah decla', Boss," said Nehemiah, "yuh sho' is uh good-lookin' man."
>
> "I am sorry I can't say the same thing about you," retorted David Wharton.
>
> "Oh, yes, Boss, yuh could," Nehemiah laughed out, "yuh could, ef yuh tole ez big uh lie ez Ah did."
>
> David Wharton could not help laughing at this; he laughed before he thought. Nehemiah got his freedom (p. 15).

Another, called "Dey's Auganized," would be a suitable story to tell at an AFL-CIO convention. Ananias, a coachman proud of his ability to use a whip, could split a horsefly in pieces. One day his master suggested that he cut down a hornet's nest with the whip. " 'No, sah, Massa,' said Ananias, 'Ah ain't gwine bothah dem hornets, 'case dey's auganized' " (pp. 23-24).

A few of the others fall into the tall tale category. While most of them are amusing illustrative anecdotes with a point, some are merely amusing. A few, primarily of historical interest, would probably seem funnier to uneducated persons of the past rather than to a contemporary audience. Showing the Negro's healthy sense of humor even in slave times, some turn the joke on the Negro himself as well as on the Negro's owner. The series was made more attractive by illustrations financed by Miss Ima Hogg of Houston, a patron of literature.

Negrito, subtitled "Negro Dialect Poems of the Southwest," was published a year after the 1932 "Juneteenth" collection, but there is no basis for comparison of the two. Brewer, influenced by his early reading of Paul Laurence Dunbar, wanted to write poetry—including dialect verse. He aspired to embody the Negro soul, to capture his "emotions, aspirations, sentiments, and thoughts." In a lofty foreword, he concludes with a good point: "I have tried to capture . . . as much of all this as possible in these simple poems . . . written in the uneducated Negro's own speech . . . with which I am familiar both by inheritance and by long study" (*Negrito,* p. 14). He was encouraged by the first president of the Texas Folklore Society, Dr. L. W. Payne, who thought the verses "clearly and cleverly presented," showing the Negro of that day as having "humor, good nature, happiness, and hopeful outlook."

Some verses in the book, reminiscent of Dunbar, have only the authentic dialect and traditional patriotism to recommend them. One example is "Deah Ol' Texas":

> Deah ol' Texas wid yo' prairies
> Yo' mesquite an' prickly pear,
> Wid yo' wil' grapes an' yo' berries
> An bluebonnets ebry where—
> 'Tain't uh soul could he'p but lub yuh
> Fer yo' fresh air an' sunshine,
> Fer de blue skies up abub yuh,
> An' yo' watermelon vine (p. 33).

Of the four parts, "Negro Characters of the Southwest in Epigram" is the best. There is no sentimentality to mar the epigrams. Examples selected from many will suffice to show humor and protest, as well as the author's philosophical, psychological, and sociological comment. Humor is shown in such quatrains as "Football Player":

In football time he'd allus
Be absent fum his class—
De reason dat dey flunked 'im
He missed uh fo'wad pass (p. 22).

A masterpiece of understatement is the comment on a traditional stereotyped character, "Washer Woman":

She washes fer uh livin',
De neighbuhs calls huh fool,
But dat am how huh chillun
All finished up in school (p. 26).

Brewer's name is often linked with that of Zora Neale Hurston (1901-60), a Negro writer of Florida, because they were both successful in collecting and publishing Negro folklore. Those misguided critics who marred Miss Hurston's last days by calling her "a handkerchief head," as she put it, will never make the mistake of labeling Brewer "an Uncle Tom" if they consider his "protest" verse of the 1940's.

In *Crisis Magazine*'s national poetry contest, in May, 1941, in which nine prizes were given, Brewer won third prize with "Bewilderment," in which a Negro speaks:

I do not know my way about yet in my native land;
Sometimes I sit among the crowd when often I should stand.
Ofttimes when I attend a show and "America" is played,
I sit there in the balcony, unmovable—afraid. . . .
. . . .
And even though I stand erect when "Stars and Stripes" pass by,
I know deep down within my soul my standing is a lie . . . (p. 162).

"Too Far Trip," a poem included in a privately published volume entitled *More Truth Than Poetry* (1947), was set in San Antonio. In it a father relates the experience of taking his son to see the Alamo. After viewing "the sacred building," he takes his son to the zoo, where an ironical and touching scene occurs.

The five-year-old boy is given a nickel to ride a Shetland pony, but the keeper looks at him sharply and says: " 'This ain't for you.' " The boy says nothing.

> He looked up at the keeper,
> And hung his proud head down
> And took a pocket mirror out
> And saw that he was brown (p. 17).

The poem is probably autobiographical, for Brewer was the father of a young son at that time. In "Bewilderment" the poet is not the speaker, but he shows understanding of one who is not "wholeheartedly devoted" to the symbols of democracy because of "blind hatred." The poem was prophetic in expressing the views of many groups today, but Brewer was too much of a scholar to be deterred by bitterness. He did understand it, however, and expressed it in a few poems.

In 1933, the same year his book of poems appeared, Brewer read a paper at the Waco meeting of the Texas Folklore Society on "Old-Time Negro Proverbs," sayings taken from the conversation of ex-slaves and elderly Negroes of the Southwest. They were published in the Society's eleventh volume, *Spur-of-the-Cock* (1933). Brewer wrote that "the pithiest and most savory proverbs seem to have come directly out of the Negro's own wisdom as well as environment" (p. 100). Dating back to slavery days, the proverbs are sometimes subtle, and Brewer explains them for modern readers.

"*Yuh mought as well die wid de chills ez wid de fever*" referred not only to an illness but for the slaves meant " 'You might as well get killed trying to escape as to remain a slave and die in slavery.' " "*Don' crow tel yuh git out o' de woods; dey mought be uh beah behin' de las' tree*" was an obscure way of saying " 'Don't be careless about talking to people you see, until you get to the Underground Railway. You might get caught and returned to your owner.' " "*Don' say no mo' wid yo' mouf dan yo' back kin stan'* " admonished the slaves "to speak briefly and seldom, not only to the master but to other slaves" (p. 102).

Some of the proverbs prove that folk wisdom is ageless. College students would understand these samples immediately: "*Evah bell yuh heah ain't uh dinnah bell*" or "*Evahbody say 'goodnight' ain't gone home.*" Professors may still ponder this one: "*You got eyes to see and wisdom not to see,*" while moralists may philosophize about another analogy: "*Dirt show up de quickes' on de cleanes' cotton*" (pp. 102-04). This is Brewer's briefest collection, but it is, as a whole, interesting and witty.

After several minor publications, Brewer's next significant volume was *Humorous Folktales of the South Carolina Negro*, published in 1945. It is a collection of tales dealing with masters and slaves, the farm, the school, the church, and the railroad. Varying in quality, some tales are amusing anecdotes. One is "Thomas E. Miller's Answer to Ben Tillman." Miller was a Negro in the South Carolina Constitutional Convention of 1890 who made a famous reply to Tillman's remark: " 'Why, you dirty black rascal, I'll swallow you alive.' " Miller retorted: " 'If you do, you'll have more brains in your belly than you've got in your head' " (p. 7). This is a "traveling anecdote," also heard in other states. The Carolina tales are similar to some in Texas for an obvious reason: the settlers of East Texas, white and colored, migrated from and through the Deep South.

One section offers jokes on the ignorance of some Negroes, showing that the Negro can laugh at himself. "Little Ernest's Grammar Lesson" is representative. Trying to teach Ernest to conjugate in the negative, the teacher had him repeat over and over again, " 'I'm not going, you're not going, they're not going.' " Finally, after ten minutes, she said, " 'Ernest, don't you understand it yet?' " " 'Yessum,' " replied Ernest, " 'Ah understands it now; dey ain't nobody gwine' " (p. 23).

A group called "Question and Answer Tall Tales of Negro School Children" constitutes the most original section. Brewer says he printed the actual language of the school children who collected these sayings. They are all in the form of a question and an answer.

> What de lowest person you ever saw?
> De lowest person Ah done ever saw kin sit on a dime with his feet hangin' down.
>
> What de shortest man you done seen?
> De shortest man Ah done seen took a ladder to climb a grain o' sand.
>
> What is de tallest man you ever seen?
> De tallest man Ah ever seen was gittin' a haircut in Heaven an' a shoeshine in Hell.
>
> What de blackest baby you done ever saw?
> De blackest baby Ah done ever saw, his mamma was carrin' 'im up de street an' de policeman arrest her for carrin' a blackjack (pp. 27-28).

The use of hyperbole, illustrated here, was developed into a fine art by some Negro tale tellers. Miss Hurston referred to this type in her collections as "big old lies," which were enjoyed immensely for their imagination and humor.

Another type of folk humor, a sort of play on words, attracted wide readership when reprinted in a popular anthology edited by B. A. Botkin. A Negro farmer, after moving to the city, declines to go back to share-cropping because there were too many "ups" in it. When questioned about the "ups," he explains to the land owner:

> Well, when Ah goes to bed at night, de first thing in de mawnin' Ah got to wake UP; then Ah got to git UP; then Ah got to dress UP—go to the lot an' feed UP. Ah can't let de Mule stan' dere so Ah haf to say git UP; time Ah done work all de summer an' gather UP ma crop an' sell it here Ah come to you to settle UP; you gits yo' pencil out an' figger UP an' say to me, "Ah'm sorry but you done eat it UP." Naw, suh, Ah don't think Ah'll try it (pp. 47-48).

When the Negro folktale is mentioned, many people can think only of Uncle Remus and the Bre'r Rabbit tales. Joel Chandler Harris found that the Negro brought to the New World his ancient habit of storytelling as a pastime. In the antebellum

South, animal stories were considered a harmless way to entertain the master's children. "That the folk tales of these Negro slaves were actually projections of personal experiences and hopes and defeats in terms of symbols appears to have gone unnoticed," Arna Bontemps wrote in *The Book of Negro Folklore*. To the slave, Bre'r Rabbit had additional meaning; the theme of many of the tales concerned weakness overcoming strength through cunning.

Brewer, in a story collection called "John Tales," published in *Mexican Border Ballads and Other Lore*, the 1946 anthology of the Texas Folklore Society, called attention to a similar but less well known type of tale. In these non-animal tales, the folk hero is John, whose exploits fit into the familiar trickster theme. Constantly surprised in wrong-doing by the Colonel, the plantation owner—or a constable, judge, or someone in authority—John would attempt to clear himself by his wits. He did not always succeed, but the happy ending was when he avoided punishment or obtained a reward. As Miss Hurston put it in *The Book of Negro Folklore*, "John had numerous scrapes and tight squeezes, but he usually came out like Bre'r Rabbit. When Old Massa won, the thing ended up in a laugh just the same—a recognition that life is not one-sided" (p. 98). The storytellers could poke fun at themselves as well as their masters, but "pretentiousness was unfailingly exposed."

In Brewer's twenty-one tales of this genre, the setting is the South before or just after the Civil War, when Negroes gained luxuries by their wits. In the first group of tales, John outwits the old Colonel and gets the chicken he wants or keeps the watermelon he has "borrowed." One day he decides he is tired of eating 'possum and is going to kill a sheep. He enters the pen and knocks a sheep on the head. As he is preparing to hit another sheep, he hears footsteps. Looking up to find Colonel Clemons approaching, he shouts loudly, " 'Ah ain't gonna let no daw-gone sheep butt me to death' " (p. 85).

Once the Colonel bets John five dollars that he cannot count the hogs in his pen, and John gets a little boy to help—but there is a slipup. The boy sees that there are eight hogs in the pen and teaches John how to count them, but the excitement of winning the five dollars causes John to forget how to add them up. He hurriedly counts for the Colonel, " 'Dis one an' dat one, an' dat one an' dis one, de ol' black sow, two more an' another one' " (p. 84).

John's friend McGruder is not as clever as he is, and John takes advantage of the fact. He meets McGruder, who comes in late after having "been out hustlin'."

> "What did you git?" said John.
>
> "Chickens," replied McGruder. "Guess how many Ah's got in dis sack, and Ah'll give you both of 'em."
>
> "Two," said John.
>
> "Humph," said McGruder, "somebody musta tol' you" (p. 93).

McGruder has a wife who is also not very bright and is not religious either. One Saturday the preacher comes to talk to her and try to persuade her to join the church:

> "Sister Susan, how about comin' an' goin' to Heaben wid me?"
>
> "Well, Ah don't know," replied Susan. "McGruder been talkin' 'bout goin' up to Arkansaw dis week; if'n he don't go up there Ah might go wid yuh."
>
> "Sister," continued the preacher, "you kinda livin' in de dark, ain't yuh?"
>
> "Yeah," replied Susan, "Ah been tellin' McGruder to git de Colonel to put some windows in de cabin but he ain't never did hit" (p. 97).

On rare occasions, the joke is on John: his wit does not always get him off the hook. The best example of this is called "John and the Two White Men in Court." John and two white men are brought into court to be tried for stealing. John is unable to think of an excuse and is very nervous. When he finds out that they are going to try the white men first, he plans to listen to their stories and imitate them.

> The first case called was that of one of the white hands who was accused of stealing a horse.
>
> "Guilty, or not guilty," said the Judge.
>
> "Not guilty," replied the man; "I've owned that horse ever since he was a colt." The case was dismissed.
>
> Then the Judge called the second white man to the stand. He was accused of stealing a cow. "Guilty, or not guilty," asked the Judge.
>
> "Not guilty," replied the defendant; "I've owned that cow ever since she was a calf." The case was dismissed.
>
> Then John was called to the stand. He was accused of stealing a wagon.
>
> "Guilty, or not guilty," demanded the Judge.
>
> "Not guilty," replied John. "Ah's owned dat wagon ever since it was a wheelbarrow" (p. 101).

While not as familiar to the present generation, John served well for a time as a folk hero, and his exploits are still remembered with pleasure by the old storytellers. "Too bad you young folks done got shamed of the things that brought us through," an old lady named Shady Ann Sutton bristled at a Negro tale collector. Sometimes John may clown enough to look ridiculous, but there is something deeper behind it all. Usually he is "loping on off from the Tar Baby with a laugh." Like folk heroes since King Arthur, John was a "hopebringer."

In his early little book, *The Negro in Texas History,* Brewer gives the dates of "The Era of Slave Labor" as 1821-65. He relates that the first cargo of slaves was actually sold into Texas in the year 1821. Prior to that year Texas was a wilderness, and there was no particular need for slaves. Stephen F. Austin at that time obtained a grant from the Mexican government to settle a colony of three hundred families. The settlement was established at the present site of Old Washington-on-the-Brazos in Washington County. The first slaves in Texas toiled there and so did their descendants.

Negro slaves labored in the early development of Texas in clearing forests and cultivating cotton and rice. These early settlements were located in the Trinity, Sabine, Neches, and Colorado river bottoms. Some of the most fertile soil in America was to be found in these sections, making slave labor very profitable.

It was to these river bottoms, especially the Brazos River bottom, that Brewer went to collect folktales from the descendants of the slaves and their masters. Several years of research and collecting produced three major volumes. Other than "Juneteenth," the three major collections of Brewer's Texas folklore were published in 1953, 1956, and 1958. These are Brewer's significant contributions to the folklore and literature of the Southwest and on them his reputation stands.

In 1953 The University of Texas Press published *The Word on the Brazos*, subtitled "Negro Preacher Tales from the Brazos Bottoms of Texas." Texas historian Walter Prescott Webb called it "the best of its sort ever." It was widely reviewed as "a classic" in the field of American folk literature, and *The San Francisco Chronicle*, among other periodicals, reported that "J. Mason Brewer can rank with any folklorist, regardless of skin pigmentation."

In the introduction to *The Word on the Brazos*, Brewer reports that the Negroes who live along the river bottoms refer to the Bible as "The Word," always with reverence. However, they are frequently irreverent when telling of the preachers and their congregations, and their "pleasure in telling and listening to these tales accounts for their survival" (*The Word on the Brazos*, p. 5).

"Preacher tales," Brewer points out, are traditional in literature from the "exempla" of Chaucer's time, based on life in the Middle Ages, down to the present. They are especially prominent in oral tradition, as many current jests and anecdotes well illustrate. The Church was very powerful in Europe during the Middle Ages, and as a result its representatives were often the victims of satire and ironic stories. The Negro preacher of the post-Civil War period was a powerful figure, venerated and feared; consequently, he, too, was "put in his place" with comic anecdotes. While Brewer's collection of tales lacks the moralizing of those of antiquity, it maintains one vital characteristic—the ability to entertain.

In general, Brewer says, the preacher tales of the Negro "included both stories told by preachers in the pulpit and those related about preachers" (p. 2). Those stories told about preachers when they were *not* in the pulpit find them when they are most human. Brewer's collection is even broader in scope, involving members of the congregation. Regardless of whether they were borrowed, adapted, or created, these stories took root in the Texas river bottoms and became a part of the cultural heritage of the local folk. Brewer obtained them, he said, from "elderly Negroes and other tradition-bearers in various Brazos Bottom localities," but time is rapidly erasing these tales from the memories of the inhabitants:

> Today, in the Brazos Bottoms, few vestiges of the old plantation life remain. The times that these tales tell about have almost passed into oblivion. Many farms formerly occupied by master and slave, boss-man and sharecropper, and later by Negro farm managers and field-hands, are today occupied by Italians, Germans, Poles and other relative newcomers, who manage and work them. Yet, in spite of all changes, cotton, sugar cane and corn fields up and down the Brazos are still worked by Negroes. The original Brazos Bottom Negro has left his tracks in the soil, enriched it with his dust, and flavored it with what we call, in a broad sense, his culture (p. 5).

J. Frank Dobie, in a preface called "A Word on *The Word*," says that Brewer's earlier "Juneteenth" tales and those in *The Word* are complementary, "both in sociological values and in charm." Dobie considered the earlier tales one of the three "freshest, most original, and most significant" contributions made to the Publications of the Texas Folklore Society during his twenty-year editorship. He admired *The Word* for "the naiveté, the simplicity, the faith, the charm of this literalness." The Sister Floras and Elder Wallers of Brewer's tales are so well drawn that they will need no more explanations to future generations than Chaucer's Wife of Bath and Pardoner. For "when human beings are transplanted right off the ground into print they ' 'splain dere selfs.' "

Brewer records the tales with considerable art, as Dobie noted. Simplicity and "the charm of literalness" are seen in the conclusion of the volume's first story, called "The Preacher and His Farmer Brother." The preacher says: " 'Sid, youse got a putty good cane patch, by de he'p of de Lawd.' " The farmer replies " 'Yeah, but you oughta seed hit when de Lawd had it by Hisse'f' " (p. 10).

The omnipotent preacher is often on the receiving end of the tales' satire. Sometimes his ignorance is satirized. In one tale an educated preacher offers to teach uneducated pastors a course in theology. He wants to start by teaching *reading, writing,* and *arithmetic.* They object until he changes the outline of the course to read: "heabunly articulation, Biblical recordin', an' ecclesiastical calculation" (p. 26).

Irony and satire dominate *The Word,* but the main virtue of the book is the anecdote, well told. One anecdote, often heard in East Texas, deals with a group of children who decide to play Baptising, using a cat and her kittens for converts. They do all right with the kittens, but the cat is stubborn. An imaginary deacon asks: " 'Brothuh Pastuh, what we gonna do wid dis heah convert what 'fuse to be 'mersed?' " The imaginary pastor replies, " 'Aw, dat's awright. Jes' sprinkle her an' let her go on to hell' " (p. 43).

The "Mefdis" and "Baptis" were the largest churches among the Brazos Bottom Negroes, but other denominations were there, too, as is apparent in a dream of going to heaven as related by "Elduh Campbell what pastuh de chu'ch down to de Ole Liendo Plannuhtation." As the preacher reported to his congregation, when he arrived before the heavenly throne he first looked around:

"Ah looked to de rat an' dere was de Camelites; Ah looked to de lef' an' dere was de Mefdis's; Ah looked in de front, an' dere was de Prespuhteeruns. But Ah don' chance to see de Baptis's nowhars; so Ah flies up to whar Gawd was settin' on his th'one an' curtsies to 'im an' say, 'Gawd, whar's de Baptis' folks? Ah ain't seed 'em no place.'

"So Gawd look 'roun' behin' 'im an' say, 'Don' you see 'em back dere 'hin' mah th'one, settin' on de flo'? Dey's so devlish, dey tells so many lies, dey do's so many mean tricks till Ah haf to keep 'em rat heah 'hin' me whar Ah kin put mah han's on 'em an' keep 'em straight' " (pp. 82-83).

The "amen" corner was a vigorous one in most Brazos Bottom churches, and most preachers enjoyed the loud responses from the good sisters—but not always. Once a preacher was in the middle of a sermon " 'bout de good-for-nothin' young generation." He said, " 'Yeah, dey's goin' to hell in Cadillacs; . . . dey's goin' to hell in Dodges.' " One sister jumps up and says, " 'Well, mah boy'll be back, 'caze he's goin' in a T-model Fo'd' " (p. 85).

Not all the satire here is directed at the preachers or their congregations. Following the ancient custom of satirizing persons in power, one old man tells the story of Uncle Si and the Bossman, reminiscent of the earlier collection of the "John Tales." Uncle Si, with his large family, sharecrops, but he never comes out ahead at the end of the year:

When Unkuh Si go up to Colonel Wilson's house evuh yeah at settlement time de Colonel 'ud say, "Well, Unkuh Si, lemme see: you got fawty gallons of sorghums; 'bout eighty yaa'ds of calico, gingham an' percale; fifty-eight pair of brogan shoes; twelve pair of duckins, thuty-six jars of snuff, six barrels of sugah, fifteen barrels of flour, a hundred plugs of chewin' tobackuh, fo' dozen pair of black cotton stockin's, five dozen pair of socks, ten bottles of castuh oil, lebun boxes of Black Draf', seventy poun's of dry salt bacon, ten sacks of navy beans, an' 'bout twenty-five work hats."

> When de Colonel git thoo readin' off dis list, he'd say, "Unkuh Si, yo' bill am settled; you don' owe me nothin'" (p. 92).

One year, however, Uncle Si demands a receipt.

> "A receipt?" yell de Colonel; "cain't you teck mah word for hit? Ain't Ah been dealin' fair wid you all dese yeahs?"
>
> "Yas, suh, dat's awright," 'low Unkuh Si. "But Ah'm gittin' ole now, an' youse gittin' ole too, an' we mought die fo' nex' yeah dis time, when hit comes to be time for de settlement, an' when Ah gits up to heabun an' St. Peter asts me is mah bills all paid 'fo' he lets me in de heabunly gates, Ah wants a receipt to show 'im; Ah don' wanna be runnin' all ovuh hell lookin' for you" (p. 93).

In the earlier series of tales about John, his sons are shown in one tale to be as sly as the father. This volume adds one more tale of that type called "John's Trip to Hell." John, a bad little boy, gets angry and runs away one winter day because the big crowd of preachers at his house eats up all the fried chicken and gets the warmest places around the log fire. After being gone for a couple of days, he shows up when the house is again full of preachers. This dialogue takes place:

> "Hello dere, John," say Sandy. "Whar you been?"
>
> "Ah's been whar you tole me," 'low John—"to hell."
>
> "Well, how is things down dere?" say Sandy.
>
> "Jes' lack dey is heah," say John—"so many damn preachuhs 'roun' de fiah till you cain't git to hit."

Brewer tells the stories like a trained folklorist; the folk customs of the past are recorded in the language of the times. Any Southerner who has eaten ham and red-eye gravy with his grits will appreciate the description of a youngster at breakfast, "soppin' his biscuits in his 'lasses an' one-eyed gravy" (p. 16). To supplement the preacher's salary "dey pass de hat 'roun' mongst de membuhs" and the good ladies of the church "hab poun' paa'ties whar evuhbody brung a poun' o' victuals to de pastuh evuh mont' . . ." (p. 17).

One folk custom, substantiated by the result, was how to get secrets out of a sleeping preacher who was suspected of being unfaithful to his wife. A trouble-making sister advised his wife: " 'Ah tells you a good way to fin' out if'n Elduh Curry been flyin' 'roun' wid de sistuhs; when he go to sleep tonight, you git a wash pan full of cold wattuh an' hol' his lef' han' down in hit an' he'll tell you his guts' " (p. 70).

The custom of Sunday funerals is historical: "'Reckly attuh freedom, dey hab de funerals on Sunday, 'caze de boss-mens don' 'low no funerals in de week-a-days" (p. 22). On one occasion a prominent but hypocritical church member was being buried. The teller of the tales relates:

> De membuhship of de Salem Baptis' Chu'ch think Ken's a good man, 'caze he hab a fine big family an' he 'ten' chu'ch regluh as de Sundays come. De pastuh think he a good Christun, too. So when he git up to preach Ken's funeral, he tell 'bout what a good man Brother Ken was, 'bout how true he was to his wife, an' what a good providuh he done been for his family an' all lack dat. He keep on an' he keep on in dis wise, but Ken's wife Sadie know de pastuh done errored; so she turn to de ol'es' boy, Jim, an' say, "Jim, go up dere an' look in dat coffin an' see if'n dat's yo' pappy in dere" (p. 23).

Folklorists should be grateful to the early Negro preachers for creating and preserving folk expression. J. Frank Dobie, in his foreword to *The Word on the Brazos,* comments at length on the language which Brewer preserves in the book. Dobie says that Brewer accurately records the dialect of the Negroes. There are vigorous phrases: a man may be concerned about "de sumpin'-to-eat question" or he may be on the "don'-care bandwagon." One "jes kept his potato trap shet an' don' say a mumblin' word." Some people, too ignorant to "know big wood from brush," might end up "going to hell head fo'most." There is the greedy revival traveling preacher ready to take away "some of dat good ole Brazos Bottoms cottonpickin' money," who explains his favorite part of the chicken: "Ah lacks the breas' an' all the res' " (Dobie, "A Word on *The Word*," pp. x-xi).

Brewer sets down such dialect expressions as "evuhwhichuh-whar" and "sich ca'iens-on." Descriptions of various preachers appeal to the imagination: "He preach Christ on to de cross an' off again," or "He got de runnin' off at de mouf too much." Some preachers have credentials that are in doubt. One thought he was called by the Lord when he saw the letters "G.P.C." in the sky. He took it to mean "Go Preach Christ'anity." After trial sermons, it was suggested to him that the Lord obviously meant "Go Pick Cotton" (p. 70).

Times have changed along the Brazos River, according to one tale-teller: "Sich ca'iens-on ain't in de Bottoms today." Much of the "bad religion" has changed to "good religion" and there are other signs of progress. "Mos' evuhbody got Good Religion in de Bottoms nowadays. De white folks ebun done got hit mo' so'n dey use to. White folks gittin' mo' lack black folks evuh day an' black folks gittin' mo' lack white folks evuh day. De white folks in de Bottoms sho' a long sight better'n dey was reckly attuh 'mansuhpation" (p. 61).

While collecting those preacher tales in the Brazos Bottoms, Brewer ran across some anecdotes on snuff-dipping, an ancient habit. One tells of the Sunday that "Elduh" Waller preached a sermon entitled "Who Can Go to Heaven" and encountered some opposition in the congregation. The concluding dialogue, as Brewer records it, is an amusing comment on human nature. The preacher is in the midst of his strong sermon:

> He say, "None of you liahs, you cain't git in." "Tell de truf!" shout Sistuh Flora. "None of you gamblers, you cain't git in," say de Elduh. "Speak outen yo' soul!" squall Sistuh Flora. "None of you whiskey drinkers, you cain't git in," say Elduh Waller. "Tell de truf!" shout Sistuh Flora. "None of you snuff dippers," say Elduh Waller, "you cain't git in," an' when he say dis heah, Sistuh Flora what got her mouf full of snuff rat den, jump up an' p'int her

finguh in Elduh Waller's face an' say, "Wait a minnit, Bub; you bettuh say, not ez you knows of" (p. 85).

This anecdote gave Brewer an idea for his next book. Three years later, in 1956, he published a limited edition of four hundred copies of a beautifully bound book which was attractive in appearance and content. Entitled *Aunt Dicy Tales,* it contained fourteen "snuff-dipping tales of the Texas Negro." A tale similar to the above anecdote illustrates the difference, as well as the similarity, of the two volumes. Aunt Dicy is the protagonist here, as the title suggests; and she becomes annoyed with her pastor. As Brewer concludes the tale:

> when Reverend Jackson got up to preach he started out as usual listing the kind of people who were going to Hell. "All you drunkards," he said, "You're going to lift your eyes in Hell one of these mornings; all of you liars, you're going to lift your eyes in Hell one of these mornings; all of you gamblers, you're going to lift your eyes in Hell one of these mornings; and all of you snuff-dippers, too," he continued, "you're going to lift your eyes in Hell one of these mornings." And when Reverend Jackson said this Aunt Dicy jumped straight up from the bench she was sitting on and yelled, "Look ahere, Reverend, you've done stopped preaching and gone to meddling now" (p. 46).

Aunt Dicy, of course, is a figure of the past. Even the use of snuff is considered a folk custom of the past by the present generation, but few of us realize how far into the past it really goes. In his introduction to *Aunt Dicy Tales* Brewer gives the historical background of tobacco and snuff beginning with pre-historic times, proceeding to the present, then predicting that snuff-dipping will continue for a long time in the future. He tells us that Columbus brought a Spanish monk named Ramón Pane to the New World when he made his second voyage. Pane wrote of the Indians' habit of "snuffing" powdered tobacco leaves into the nose through a tube in his study of their customs, called *De Insularium Ritibus* (Customs of the Islanders), in 1497. A later work by Oviedo, *Historia de Las Indias* (1526), tells about the Indians "sniffing tobacco through the nostrils by means of a forked tube" (*Aunt Dicy Tales*, p. 2). "Snuff," later to be dipped instead of sniffed, thus has indeed an ancient history. It may not be sniffed in the Southwest today, but it is still being dipped.

Brewer also mentions in his introduction that in 1612 the American colonists began cultivating the tobacco plant and that in 1619 a Dutch man-of-war sold twenty Negroes to the plantation owners in Jamestown. Thus, Brewer concludes, "the Negro's entrée on the American scene and the beginning of the American tobacco industry became synonymous" (p. 3). Ironically, the relationship between Negroes and snuff continues to this day. A large amount of snuff is sold each year in the South and Southwest, and Texas is its largest consumer. Brewer was convinced, in the decade of the 1950's, that the majority of the people who bought snuff regularly were Negroes (p. 8). The use of snuff by Negroes in Texas in the period following the Civil War has provided the subject matter for his most unusual book. Brewer intended for the snuff-dipping narratives not only to "give the reader an insight into the sharp and inherent homespun humor of the American Negro, but provide him with stimulating entertainment as well" (p. 9).

Brewer sets the scene for the stories with an introduction to Aunt Dicy and her snuff-dipping neighbors. "Immediately after the Negro slaves in Texas were freed," he writes, "Aunt Dicy Johnson of Lee County had the name of being the biggest snuff-dipper in the whole state" (p. 10). Most of her neighbors dipped snuff too, for a variety of reasons. Aunt Cindy Wilson dipped when she was going to whip her children, for it gave her extra power to whip them with. And Big Tim Collins used it to kill his hunger when picking cotton; instead of stopping for dinner, Big Tim took a dip of snuff and was able to pick two or three hundred more pounds a day. Uncle Jonas Jennings used snuff as preventive medicine; before he took up the habit he suffered from all sorts of complaints, but afterwards, he never had a sick day in his life.

Another of Aunt Dicy's neighbors, Aunt Rosa Clemmons, used snuff to keep her teeth clean; and to prove it, all she had to do was open her mouth, revealing pretty white teeth which gleamed in the sunshine (pp. 10-11).

Last, with perhaps the most effective testimony on the virtues of snuff, was Little Joe Washington. Little Joe was only four feet tall, and all the big men in town picked on him. One Saturday they all started jumping on him at the general store. Little Joe turned to the counter and bought a can of snuff, took a few dips, and then was able to knock one of the men down nine times. Little Joe said that the snuff gave him strength and made him brave. He kept on dipping it for the rest of his life, and the men never bothered him again (p. 11).

Aunt Dicy dipped snuff simply because she liked to. She dipped more than any of her neighbors and kept up the habit for as long as she lived. She was not ashamed of dipping and did not care who knew she dipped—except for the preacher, who finally found out about it. But even his knowing did not make Aunt Dicy stop dipping snuff (p. 11).

Texas naturalist Roy Bedichek, widely noted as a man of letters, wrote a foreword for the volume. He felt that the Aunt Dicy stories were skillfully written humorous pioneer tales which, besides telling about snuff-dipping, also contained some homey situations, giving us a view of the social history of settlers in south central Texas counties, "enlivened with descriptions of quaint folkways, folk talk and folk beliefs" (p. ix). Bedichek particularly admired the character portrayal of Aunt Dicy, a personality built around a single vice—snuff dipping. He found her an endearing character who was neither negative, mealy-mouthed, nor wishy-washy. "She takes a stand and stands by it. She dominates each situation as it arises, while her one vice seems to throw her virtues into sharper relief" (p. ix).

Bedichek cites as a case of Aunt Dicy's individualism her reaction to Booker T. Washington's speech in Austin on "Great Americans and Their Contributions." The speech was highly praised by all hearers except Aunt Dicy, who complained that he did not mention Levi Garrett the snuff maker—"he wasn't nobody's fool" (p. x). Bedichek wrote that

> to take a stand for good and sufficient reasons and to maintain it against the mass- or herd-opinion, indicates that quality of character we call the "courage of non-conformity," itself a sign of spiritual strength. The "courage of one's convictions" is the basis, also, of the virtue of loyalty, so highly prized in its purer forms—*i.e.*, unadulterated with self-interest—because it is so exceedingly rare (p. x).

J. Frank Dobie agreed with Bedichek and praised the book in reviews and in his newspaper columns. While not told in dialect, the tales have "the right tune," Dobie said. The dialect comes through in the crayon drawings of John T. Biggers, a well-known Negro artist. The drawings illustrate Aunt Dicy's dress, character, and spirit; other drawings show snuff, snuff salesmen, and other people. "The tales illustrate the drawings as much as the drawings illustrate the tales," Dobie wrote.

One of the snuff-dipping tales included in the collection gives the origin of the place-names Dime Box and Old Dime Box near Yegua Creek in Lee County. There are a number of theories about the origin of these names, but Brewer's is one of the most interesting because he ties it to the "one vice" of Aunt Dicy Johnson. Late in her life, she moved far into the country, too far to walk to the general store. But have snuff she must; therefore, she contrived a plan to have it brought to her:

> Every Saturday, from that time on, as long as Aunt Dicy lived on the Schultze farm she would meet the mailman and give him a dime to bring her a dime box of snuff. Everybody in the little community knew about Aunt Dicy's practice of sending for snuff by the mailman, so they called a meeting one night and decided to call the little community "DIME BOX OF SNUFF" in honor of Aunt Dicy. They shortened it later to just "Dime Box" and to this day, this little community still goes by the name of DIME BOX (p. 18).

The character of Aunt Dicy as well as the humor of this collection can be illustrated by one tale, "Aunt Dicy in the Courtroom." Aunt Dicy's son Pomp had just finished high school when he got into some trouble with the sheriff over shooting dice and was forced to stand trial. Aunt Dicy went to the courthouse to pay Pomp's fine, but she was so upset when she left home that she forgot to take along a bag to spit snuff-juice in. So when she got ready to spit, she had to do it on the floor of the courtroom. When one of her neighbors saw her spit on the floor, he went over to her to ask her whether she knew there was a five dollar fine for it:

> "No! I didn't, Son," replied Aunt Dicy taking three "five dollar" bills out of an old handkerchief in which she carried her money, "so I tell you what you do; take this fifteen dollars and give it to the Judge for me right now, 'cause I'm going to spit two more times before I leave the Court House" (p. 42).

This unique volume of authentic social history and genuine folktales is probably the only collection of snuff-dipping tales published in the English language. A collector's item, it has a place, the author tells me, in the private libraries of such diverse personalities as Queen Elizabeth of England, the late Eleanor Roosevelt, Dwight D. Eisenhower, and Allan Shivers, ex-governor of Texas.

Brewer's third and best of the major volumes published in Texas is entitled *Dog Ghosts and Other Texas Negro Folk Tales* (1958). Along with the snuff-dipping tales, the ghost stories, in which the ghost is a dog, seem to be among Brewer's most original contributions to the literature of the Southwest.

The title *Dog Ghosts* applies to only nine stories in a collection of sixty-three. They are the most unusual but not necessarily the most interesting. The ghosts are benign spirits in the form of a large white dog with red eyes. Thrown rocks would go "clean thoo hit," and it appears or disappears in a puff of smoke. All such ghosts return to aid or protect loved ones. All—except one case of "a Christian friend"—are members of the family which it aids. Three mothers return to comfort their children. A wife returns to help her husband. A first wife returns to pull her "breeches quilt" off the stepmother's bed in Greenville and cover her children. A father returns to keep his wayward son from getting his throat cut. Another father, Hamlet-like, returns to defend his son from an evil uncle. A third father returns, in true ghost tradition, to show his penniless family where his money is hidden.

The other nine tales in this section are of the traditional ghost variety—two involve a "haidless hossman," one ghost is a tap dancer who keeps tap-tap-tapping in his coffin, and one is a jealous-old-man ghost who plans to haunt the "Black Widow Car" of his young wife "if'n she coa'ts o' rema'ies." Perhaps the best-named ghost in Texas is one who calls himself Sifty-Sifty San'. Cars, antique beds, sawmill bridges, two-story houses, and oil fields are haunted by white or Negro ghosts. The McManor Bridge Ghost, near Camden, originated when "a mean ole white man, Dave McManor, what used to own a saw-mill, an' whip de Nigguhs what was wuckin' at his saw-mill when dey ain't wuck to suit 'im, was killed at de spot whar de bridge covuhs a li'l' stream of wadduh" (p. 115). His horse "th'owed" him and left him "daider'n a door knob." He did not quite equal the ghost of Brit Bailey, a colorful character who "lef' word in his will dat he wanted to be buried stannin' up wid his pistol in one han' an' his lantern in t'othuh one, an' a jug of whiskey at his feet" (p. 123). It was Brit, of course, who set gas afire and blew up an oilfield when it got too close to Bailey's Prairie where he walked at night.

The additional forty-four tales in the volume illustrate the variety of Brewer's earlier publications. The other four sections are "Slavery and Its Legacy," more master and slave tales; "Carefree Tales," more humorous anecdotes; "Tales of Animals and Ranch Life," some in the Uncle Remus tradition; and "Religious Tales," reminiscent of Brewer's collection of preacher tales.

The tales from the days of slavery usually concern a trick played on the master by the slave, or vice versa. One, whose moral concerns the frequent hypocrisy of those who pray the loudest, is about Uncle Israel and his loud, nightly prayer for the Lord "to come an' git 'im an' ca'ie 'im home to heabun, whar he kin feas' on milk an' honey, an' res' his weary bones" (p. 17). The plantation owner overhears him and decides to play a trick on him. He interrupts the prayer with a loud knock and announces that he, the Lord, has come to answer the request. Uncle Israel demurs, and the joke is repeated the next night. Again Uncle Israel delays. On the third night he reveals that he is not exactly as religious as he has pretended to be:

> "Lawd," 'low Unkuh Israel, a-sweatin' an' a-pantin' for bref, but not budgin' a inch from de chimley cawnuh; "Ah done tol' you three times now dat Ah wasn't ready to go to heabun yit, so go on 'way from heah now an' lemme 'lone! Ah see now why de Jews kilt you; youse so damn haa'd-haided!" (p. 18).

The tables are turned in the story of "Uncle Jasper's Prayer." Uncle Jasper is praying under "de Prayer Tree" when he is overheard and reported by the master's son. The master thinks it amusing to hide in the tree and pretend to be the Lord. When Jasper asks for a gift from heaven—"a wadduh bucket full of sweet 'taters, an' a big domineckuh chicken"—the "Lord" advises him to come tomorrow night and pray again. The next night Uncle Jasper arrives singing:

> "One of de sweetes' things in life
> Am de uncloudy welcome of a wife" (p. 16).

He knows his wife most desires a Sunday dinner of "sweet 'tater cobbler an' baked chicken." The master drops the gifts down to Uncle Jasper, but his satisfaction is short-lived. The master "don' know dat Unkuh Jasper done recognize his voice de night 'fo' an' know dat he playin' lack he be de Lawd . . . so he rail surprised when Unkuh Jasper raise his eyes up to'a'ds de tree-top an' say,

'Lawd, Ah sho thanks you for dese sweet 'taters an' dis chicken, ebun if you did sen' 'em by de Devul' " (p. 17).

The section called "Carefree Tales" begins with a quotation from one of the humorous anecdotes, and a character tells, in brief, how he manages to be carefree: " 'Ah don' dig up de pas', and Ah don' tote de future'." There follow amusing tales of Juneteenth-fishing, "whoppin' big lies," 'possum peddling, and bootlegging. The well-known character of the bootlegger is introduced poetically:

He sell hit to de rich;
He sell hit to de po'es';
He sell hit to de ones
What pay him de mo'es'.

He sell hit to de black,
He sell hit to de white;
He sell hit in de daytime,
An' he sell hit come night (p. 37).

The first and best of the series is called "The Hays County Courthouse Janitor." Sug Miller, it seems, had been a janitor in San Marcos for twenty-five years and never missed a day coming to work. He was fired, however, when a new judge decided he wanted a janitor who could read and write. Sug, working just as hard on a farm as he had at the courthouse, soon owned it. Four years later the judge drove by and admired Sug's fields of cotton, corn, sugar cane, as well as his chickens, turkeys, hogs, and cows. The story ends with this dialogue:

"Sug, you sho hab come up in de worl' fas'—tain't no tellin' what you'd of been sho 'nuff, if'n you'd of knowed how to read an' write."

"Ah knows zackly what Ah'd of been," 'low Unkuh Sug; "Ah'd of still been de janitor at de Hays County Coa't-house" (p. 26).

The animal tales here often end with a moral as is usual in this prevalent genre of the Negro's oral tradition. The first in the series is a good illustration. A young West Texas boy hears his minister preach on the subject of "treatin' all God's critters right." As he walks home after church remembering the sermon, he picks up a rattlesnake that has been frozen in the winter ice on the ground. He warms the snake inside his jacket; and as it thaws out, it prepares to strike, surprising the boy:

> "Mistuh Snake—you mean to tell me you gonna bite me attuh Ah done done what de preachuh say do an' teck you in mah bosom an' done waa'm you nex' to mah body?"
>
> An' de snake say, "Hell, yeah, Nigguh; you knowed Ah was a snake when you picked me up, didn' you?" (p. 46).

The "Religious Tales" treat the preacher and the church members humorously, as one would expect from the author of *The Word on the Brazos*. "Elder Brown's False Teeth" is a satire on the Southern preacher's traditional love of chicken. When the "Revun" drops his teeth in the Brazos River, all his efforts to recover them fail. A bright young man—surely a son of Old John—thinks of a new trick.

> So li'l' Buster runned home rail fas', an' putty soon he comed back wid a big drumstick tied to de end of a cord string an' th'owed it in de wadduh rat whar Elduh Brown done say his teeth falled in de rivuh; an' you know sump'n'? No sooner'n dat cord string hit de wadduh, dem teeth jumped up an' ketched hol' of de drumstick an' li'l' Buster yanked 'em out an' han' 'em to Revun Brown sayin', "Heah's yo' teeth, Elduh" (p. 76).

Humorous social satire, applicable to prideful people of any race, is well illustrated in a tale about the members of "de Mt. Carmel Baptis' Chu'ch in Marlin." It was a "silk-stockin'" church but one poor field hand joined it. Mose was frowned on because he was so poor that he paid his dues "wid chitlins, pork ribs, an' middlin's in de wintuh time, an' wid roastin' yeahs, wadduhmelons an' sorghum 'lasses in de summuh time." The higher-class Negroes did not want him. As the narrator says: "De ones 'speshly what don' wan' 'im in de chu'ch was Doctuh

Cook, what hab a Cadillac car; de unnuhtakuh, Charlie Briggs, what hab a Packard car; de school principal, 'Fessuh Hamilton, what hab a Buick car, an' de son of a white boss-man what lib out to Ebenezer, an' own his own fawm, by de name of Jim Peterson, what hab a Dodge car" (p. 77). Mose, of course, drives an old Model T Ford. Eventually they all drive through life and on up to the Pearly Gates. St. Peter interviews each of them about the car he drives, and all of the rich men are turned away. Justice triumphs in the end:

> De las' one of 'em to die was de po' han', Mose Smith. So he driv' up to de pearly gates wid his old T-model Fo'd jes' a-rattlin' an' a-shakin' lack hit was gonna fall to pieces evuh minute de Lawd sen'! Hit kep' up so much fuss 'till bof Saint Peter an' Gawd comes runnin' up to de heabunly gates an' peeps ovuh de fence to see what keepin' up all dis heah racket at de high gates of heabun; an' when Gawd looked out an' seed Mose an' his ole rickety Fo'd a-rattlin' an' a-squeakin', he turnt to Saint Peter an' say, "Open de gate, Peter, an' let 'im in—he done had hell 'nuff!" (p. 78).

After leaving Texas, Brewer continued to publish tales and anecdotes of Negro life. Two notable collections are "North Carolina Negro Oral Narratives" in the journal *North Carolina Folklore* and the book-length *Worser Days and Better Times*. Most of the tales in the North Carolina collections are similar to those in his earlier Texas volumes. The religious anecdote, "which beyond a reasonable doubt exists in greater abundance than any other type of American Negro oral narrative," is much the same in North Carolina and Texas, Brewer says. The religious anecdote still plays a part in the life of the Negro community and maintains its position as one of the specimens of Negro anecdotal materials (*North Carolina Folklore*, IX, 22).

The type of tale very popular in the Negro community can be illustrated by one in *Worser Days and Better Times* called "The Preacher and the Board Meeting."

A country minister around Mocksville ended his sermon and then announced that he would like to have all the Board to remain for a few minutes. A stranger in the village who had worshipped at the church that morning made his way to the front pew and seated himself with the deacons and elders.

The minister approached him and said, "My dear sir, perhaps you misunderstood. I asked that only the Board remain."

"Well, that included me too," replied the stranger, " 'cause I was never mo' bored in my life" (p. 54).

Worser Days and Better Times ranges from the worse times of the past to the better days of the present. The contents are a potpourri of folk narratives including all types which the author has collected during his long career. There are folktales and anecdotes, folk sayings, superstitions, folk rhymes, and verses. It includes the most "modern" contents of all his books, showing the contemporary Negro's attitudes, aspirations, and interests.

The author has listened with a keen ear and recorded accurately what he heard. He says in the introduction that much in his previous collections had been rewritten and restyled by him, resulting in their being "something of others" and "mostly of me." But this collection, he says, is "mostly of others" and "something of me." The tales and anecdotes were heard on buses and trains, in cafes or drugstores, or while standing on street corners. "A more authentic and natural product can be obtained when the informant is unaware that what he says is being collected" (p. 25).

Although many of the tales about ministers are of a modern type, there is still the punning comedy which added pleasure to *The Word on the Brazos*. For example, in "Both Were Proud," the twin sons of a country couple go away to school and become preachers. When they return to the farm they are fed, of course, a large platter containing two "fryin'-size" chickens. After observing the dinner, the rooster in the yard turns to a hen and says, " 'Ain't you proud o' our two sons what just entered de ministry?' " (p. 46).

The section on puns and comic misunderstandings concludes with "The Spelling Bee and the County Superintendent." The dumbest boy in the class, with the unlikely name of Damn-it Jones, was not exactly a favorite of the teacher. After the other boys had failed to spell "Nebuchadnezzar," Damn-it raised his hand and asked for a chance to try. The teacher said, " 'Damn-it Jones, you can't spell it,' " to which remark the superintendent answered, " 'Hell, teacher, let him try!' " (p. 65).

The section called "Tales of the Wise and Foolish" contains many "traveling anecdotes" which are also heard in the Southwest. A unique one, "The Cherokee Indian and the Asheville Banker," is delightful but impossible to shorten enough to repeat here. Several seem to be modern-day versions of the old "John tale" cycle. John's descendants still outwit those in authority. In "The Deputy Sheriff and the Negro Bootlegger," the sheriff tries to trick the bootlegger into selling him some whiskey so that he can arrest him on the spot. The Negro asks the deputy how much whiskey he wants; and when the deputy replies, " 'About five dollars' worth,' " the bootlegger says that he will see what he can do and takes the money. Before leaving, the Negro hands the deputy sheriff a shoe box: " 'Hold these shoes for me till I git back.' " The sheriff takes the shoe box and waits for three hours, but the Negro never returns. When he opens the box, there is his fifth of bootleg whiskey (p. 66).

In "Harrison Neal and the Game Warden," it is the game warden who is fooled when the out-of-county fisherman throws a fake "lipilectic" fit. Told in a colorful dialect filled with original folk expressions, it is one of the best tales Brewer has ever recorded. The setting is in the day "when Mr. Hoover done clap de panic on" causing the vicinity to be "kivvered up wid hard times." Neal has lost his job for a week and has no money to buy food. "If'n railroad engines was a dime a dozen he ain't had 'nuff money to blow de whistle on one of 'em." He says, "De chiggers done give up on me, cause po' old Neal ain't hardly got blood 'nuff for heself. . . . my backbone feels lack it been workin' button holes in my stomach. . . . I done et so many of dem little fishes an' little birds an' little rabbits till old Neal don't know whether he spose to swim or fly or walk." In the end he outwits the game warden, catches a string of catfish, and swaps half of them to a white gardener for "a hat full of 'matoes an' cucumbers, some roasinyears, an' a cabbage or two" and has a fine meal (pp. 76-79).

One section is called "Folk Talk." What folklorists mean by folk speech is often vague, and Brewer, who has always been keenly aware of unique expressions, adds a note of explanation. People who live in the United States like to voice their opinions so that they can be heard by other people, Brewer says. And although some of the things they say are senseless, most of their talk is full of sense and meaning. Brewer points out that folk talk has just recently entered urban centers, brought by people migrating from the farms and mountains to cities and towns; and as a result of this migration "city sidewalks and buses have replaced the old time liars' benches" (p. 127).

Negro folk talk, Brewer feels, is one of the most interesting of the types of folk talk in America "because of its odd and picturesque qualities." Brewer illustrates those qualities with a quotation at the beginning of the "Folk Talk" section which explains the Negro migration from farm to city and from South to North: "I'd rather be in New York starvin' to death than to be down here with nothin' but Monday mornin', meal, molasses, mules, an' meanness" (p. 125).

The "talk" is divided into several divisions. One of each will illustrate. General Aphorisms and Observations: "Now I lay me down to sleep, a dollar down and a dollar a week—dat's de procedure." Colorful Turns and Figures of Speech: "I'm goin' to one of dem way-back-in-de-country dances an' raise me five dollars worth of hell." Religion and Faith: "He's a sho-nuff, stomp-down devil-chasin' preacher." Current Events and Race

Relations: "What was the use of the Yankees freein' us, if we wasn't gonna do nothin'?" Behavior and Etiquette: "I always kept my head up and my dress down."

The next section on superstitions (signs and charms) is a reminder of the author's early Texas collection, "Old-Time Negro Proverbs." These were collected from older adults; the younger generation of Negro college students "declare that they have no belief in superstitions at all." The most original group in the collection consists of several superstitions concerning ball games. For example, "A haircut before a game will make you weak, causing your team to lose the game." That one probably started with Samson.

The concluding section, "Folk Rhymes and Verse," reflects Brewer's interest in verse since the publication of *Negrito* in 1933. It is amusing to see what he found written in students' autograph albums. Two humorous couplets will illustrate:

> If you want your man, better keep him by your side;
> If he flags my train, I'm sure gonna let him ride.
>
> I don't make love by the garden gate,
> For love is blind, but the neighbors ain't (p. 166).

More books by Brewer are forthcoming, and no doubt his influence and reputation will grow. However, he does not have to depend upon future publications to attain distinction. Already he has done some unique collecting, writing, and publishing; he has consistently improved and matured as a writer; and he has made a permanent place for himself in the history of Southwestern literature.

His first "Juneteenth" collection alone would not have done so. A number of the tales show a kind of relationship between master and slave once romanticized by Thomas Nelson Page. In 1932, Brewer told Dobie "how unrepresentative the loudly-heralded Negro literature out of Harlem" was, "how false both in psychology and language." He meant it was false to the Southern and Southwestern Negroes, but his slave tales were also "false," in a way, to the contemporary Negro of the United States. What, then, was their value? They were certainly of historical importance, especially to those interested in folktales of the past. But their real value to Brewer and to his readers was the fact that they set Brewer to mining what was to be a rich bed of ore.

Brewer's printed poetry would not have gained much stature for him. However, his verse, as published in *Negrito* and periodicals of the day, were another forward step in his development as a writer, as was his compiling of Negro proverbs, beginning with the published collection in 1933. He became adept at recording or composing simple verses in dialect, as well as collecting proverbs which often rhymed in couplets or quatrains. His four best long works—*The Word on the Brazos, Aunt Dicy Tales, Dog Ghosts,* and *Worser Days and Better Times*—are enlivened by the frequent use of verses and proverbs within the tales. It is a vivid trademark of his style.

As he continued to write, Brewer broadened his scope to record the life, past and present, of the Negro in the Southwest and elsewhere. He believed that this life deserved representation in literature, and he hoped to arouse in his people an interest in their own artistic capabilities. His success in publishing may well bring about success in influencing others to follow his example.

Because of their subject matter and the extended use of Negro dialect in their writings, it was inevitable that Brewer should be compared to Joel Chandler Harris. He has been called "a worthy successor" to the creator of Uncle Remus. Appropriate, if ironic, is the fact that Harris' successor in this field is a *Negro* writer. A comparison today shows that Brewer's use of dialect is more genuine and colorful, his dialogue more convincing, his interpretations more valid. That is as it should be. As Brewer says of the uneducated Negroes' speech, it is "a speech with which I am familiar both by inheritance and by long study." Only a Negro could have such an unlimited opportunity to record the lore of the common folk with such exact wording, pronunciation, and style. From lifelong and intimate association with his source materials, he became a master of the colorful idiom of folk speech, with its hyperbole and simile, its invective and humor. One of his strong points is the recording and creation of folk speech full of earthy and amusing poetry—in the broadest sense of the word. While often compared to Harris, Brewer is significantly different from him in ways besides race and geography. The publication of the Uncle Remus books between 1881 and 1905 caused general acceptance of the idea that American Negro folktales were all animal stories—about Bre'r Rabbit, Bre'r Fox, and others. Since subsequent collectors who looked for Negro stories were primarily interested in animal tales, that is what they found.

White audiences long ago accepted the Negro spiritual and the Negro animal tale of the Uncle Remus sort. They were slower to accept the Negro secular song and the non-animal tale. The advent of "rhythm and blues" and "rock and roll" in the past few decades has brought the Negro secular song into prominence. Whereas the spirituals expressed the Negroes' longings, hopes, and aspirations, the blues were more frank in expressing his disillusionment with this world and his protest against things in it.

Brewer is one who has made the non-animal tale known and accepted—even those that, like some of the "blues," are frank and direct in their social criticism and protest. Another Negro folklorist who shares with Brewer the credit for bringing the non-animal tale to prominence is the late Zora Neale Hurston. They head a list of writers (and are the only well-known Negroes) of the recent decades of the twentieth century who found new kinds of folktales which earlier collectors either did not find or tended to ignore because of their concentration on animal stories. Significantly, Brewer's "Juneteenth" tales were published three years before Miss Hurston's first collection, *Mules and Men,* in 1935. Unlike Brewer, she continued to avoid any tales which contained social protest in any of her seven major works published before her death in 1960, and his publication of tales far exceeded hers in volume.

While a writer and researcher may be doing a good thing, he cannot expect the general public to praise him unstintingly. From one source or another Brewer's work has been subjected to snipings about excessive dialect, lack of scholarly footnotes comparing variations of tales, and use of subject matter unpleasing to some people in this day of integration and equal rights. His works will substantially outlast the criticism.

In the Foreword to *Dog Ghosts,* Chapman J. Milling points out that at the beginning of this century writers and scholars spent much time recording old tales, and distinguished publishing houses promoted their works. In recent years the story told in Negro dialect has gone out of style. Dialect is taboo with many leading publishing houses. To Brewer, a realistic professor of English, this seems absurd. Certainly some Negroes speak with a Harvard accent, but most of them, like most other Americans, speak in a distinct vernacular (p. xii).

Joel Chandler Harris answered criticism of Negro dialect stories in 1883 when he wrote that it would be impossible to separate his stories from the idiom in which they have been recited for generations. "The dialect is a part of the legends themselves, and to present them in any other way would be to rob them of everything that gives them vitality."

The student of the English language will find his own study enriched by the dialect preserved in Brewer's works. His philological investigations may lead him farther than just asking if the language of English people three hundred years ago was merely modified to fit the lingual peculiarities of the Southwestern Negro. When he finds *hit* for *it, ax* for *ask,* and *heap* for *a lot of people,* he may return to his reading of Chaucer and Shakespeare with some new knowledge. Far from being guilty of the abuse of dialect, Brewer has, through his attention to cadence and idiom, restored dignity to a speech that was almost ruined by sentimentality, condescension, and the grotesques of minstrel shows and early movies.

Brewer, like J. Frank Dobie, is a collector and artistic user of folklore; he leaves the scholarship to others who are specialists on origins and comparisons of versions. Harris faced a similar problem apparently, for once he let Uncle Remus say: "Dat de reason I don't like ter tell no tale ter grown folks, speshually ef dey er white folks. Dey'll take it an' put it by de side er some yuther tale what dey got in der min' . . ." (Brookes, p. xvi).

Harris once wrote in a review of some folktales of the Southwest: "First, let us have the folk-tales told as they were intended to be told, for the sake of amusement—as a part of the art of literary entertainment. Then, if the folklorists find in them anything of value to their pretensions let it be picked out and preserved with as little cackling as possible" (Brookes, p. 24). Harris, like Brewer, never got lost in the maze of ethnic investigation. Both have been content to insure that each item comes fresh and direct from the Negro source.

Brewer and Harris hold similar opinions about the origin of their tales which are not shared by all professional scholars. Harris said, "One thing is certain—the Negroes did not get them from the whites: probably they are of remote African origin" (Brookes, p. 23). Brewer says in *Dog Ghosts* that his tales "are as varied as the Texas landscape, as full of contrasts as Texas weather. Among them are tales that have their roots deeply imbedded in African, Irish, and Welsh mythology; others have parallels in pre-Columbian Mexican tradition; and a few have versions that can be traced back to Chaucer's England. Many of these stories, however, appear to be indigenous" (p. 3). In introducing his "dog spirit" tales, Brewer goes further into their African origin:

> As far as I have been able to ascertain, the dog spirit tale is not a part of any oral American tradition except that of the Negro. Its prevalence among Negroes may be explained by the widespread African myth that tells how the dog became a friend to man, helping him to catch his food, showing him the cunning ways of the wild beasts, and demanding in re-

> turn only a place by man's hearth and bones from his meals. In all of the dog spirit stories I collected in the Red River bottoms and elsewhere in Texas, the dog is a benign ghost, who appears only to help someone in distress. It is perhaps safe to speculate that these tales were first related in Texas by slaves who derived their essential elements from tales told by their African ancestors (*Dog Ghosts*, p. 3).

Academic disagreement is of little interest to the general reader. Suffice it to say that collectors like Brewer give scholars material for learned treatises.

In the ninth volume of the Texas Folklore Society, *Southwestern Lore* (1931), A. W. Eddins revealed his discovery of a body of unrecorded lore in Texas, particularly in the bottoms of the Brazos River. Mr. Eddins said, "The Negro is by nature both humorist and philosopher. In his unsophisticated manner he often sounds the depths of wisdom and reveals a knowledge of human nature truly astonishing. These conclusions he expresses in quaint fables, parables pithy with satire, and anecdotes rich in character" (p. 153). The first president of the Society, Dr. Leonidas Payne, had called for members to collect these and other folk materials while there was still time. J. Mason Brewer was one who came forward, and his collecting and publishing record now stretches over thirty-five years. It is continuing, but already he detects considerable change in what he finds. He reports that the "Old-Time Negro" with his "other-worldly preoccupations," which dominated Negro oral literature during the Slavery and Reconstruction Periods, has practically disappeared. The earlier concerns have been replaced by what he terms "reality thinking," *i.e.*, the Negro's folk narratives today concern "his hopes, his problems, his worldly observation, and his struggle to gain respectable citizenship for himself." Dr. Brewer believes that this does not mean that the Negro wants to abandon his racial identity. He is proud of the Negro's historical culture and wants to preserve it for his descendants. Integration should bring about human equality, he feels, but not loss of identity.

Humor is used in expressing the early and later philosophies. In Brewer's earliest and latest writings, we see the Negro trait of "laughing it off" by what Zora Neale Hurston calls "hitting a straight lick with a crooked stick." Such folk humor can sometimes jar readers out of their complacency, and Brewer's latest work is entirely capable of having a jarring effect. His characters are not submerged, downtrodden people. They can laugh at themselves as well as others in a mature fashion. Brewer is proud of his race and not ashamed of its past; he has been a leader in preserving a good part of it. He never tires of saying, "If we do not respect the past, the future will not respect us."

Literary history gives him credit for pioneering in writing tales of snuff-dippers and dog ghosts. He is noted for valuable collections of pre-Civil War legends of John, the folk hero; of post-War comic preacher anecdotes; and of twentieth-century supernatural tales, including dog ghosts. He has recorded vivid pictures of life in many eras, some far removed from our own. Social criticism is not the major emphasis of most of his tales, but his characters and the situations created for them are not mere pegs on which to hang their dialect and folkways. While his folktales create bursts of hearty laughter, what is most important is that he has accumulated a rich body of cultural expression which has thrown light on ways of living and ways of thinking. He has made the public aware of the Negro as a contributor to the American folk tradition.

It is generally accepted that the Uncle Remus stories head the list of American folktales. If Brewer must be compared to anyone, it is flattering that he should be compared to Joel Chandler Harris.

Dr. Stella Brewer Brookes writes in her excellent critical study, *Joel Chandler Harris—Folklorist:* "If merit be aptly appraised, to Joel Chandler Harris will always go the credit for making a section famous with legends—legends which were engrafted on Southern soil." She might have applied this statement to her own brother, John Mason, by changing "Southern" to "Southwestern." If Harris, she writes, "had done no more than give a delineation of the plantation, his place in literature would be secure. However, he did more than this—he preserved from oblivion the lore significant for an insight not only into a people but into a past" (p. 149).

The analogy with Brewer is obvious. It is a simple matter to paraphrase her concluding paragraph loosely and substitute the name of the Southwestern writer so often compared with the Southern one. To those who have the capacity to use Brewer's books—scholars of folklore, students of Southwestern literature, and readers of literature generally—there are additional values. To all "real folks" who enjoy a good laugh and who frequently must seek an antidote to tension, Brewer's books will always be a source of pleasure. Those who read even a few of the tales will find them a pleasing pastime, and they may find themselves often quoting from Brewer's collections. In his volumes there is wit, there is wisdom, there is philosophy, there is literature to be relished by this and future generations.

Selected Bibliography

PRIMARY SOURCES

BOOKS

BREWER, J. MASON, *Aunt Dicy Tales* (Austin: Privately Published, 1956).

———, *Dog Ghosts and Other Texas Negro Folk Tales* (Austin: The University of Texas Press, 1958).

———, *Humorous Folktales of the South Carolina Negro* (Orangeburg, S. C.: Claflin College Press, 1945).

———, *More Truth Than Poetry* (Austin: Privately Printed, 1947).

———, *The Negro in Texas History* (Dallas: Mathis Publishing Co., 1936).

———, *Negro Legislators of Texas* (Dallas: Mathis Publishing Co., 1935).

———, *Negrito* (San Antonio: Naylor Publishing Co., 1933).

———, *Three Looks and Some Peeps* (Salisbury, N. C.: Privately Printed, 1963).

———, *The Word on the Brazos* (Austin: The University of Texas Press, 1953).

———, *Worser Days and Better Times* (Chicago: Quadrangle Books, 1965).

ARTICLES

BREWER, J. MASON, "John Tales," *Mexican Border Ballads and Other Lore*, J. Frank Dobie, ed. Vol. XXI (Austin: Texas Folklore Society, 1946), 81-104.

———, "Juneteenth," *Tone the Bell Easy*, J. Frank Dobie, ed. Vol. X (Austin: Texas Folklore Society, 1932), 9-54. Reprinted in *Texas Folk and Folklore*, Mody C. Boatright, ed. Vol. XXVI (Austin: Texas Folklore Society, 1954), 55-66.

———, "North Carolina Negro Oral Narratives," *North Carolina Folklore*, IX (July, 1961), 21-33.

———, "Old-Time Negro Proverbs," *Spur-of-the-Cock*, J. Frank Dobie, ed. Vol. XI (Austin: Texas Folklore Society, 1933), 101-05. Reprinted, with "Juneteenth," in *Texas Folk and Folklore*, pp. 219-23.

SECONDARY SOURCES

BOOKS

Bontemps, Arna and Langston Hughes, *The Book of Negro Folklore* (New York: Dodd, Mead, and Co., 1958), pp. 65-88, 141-53.

Botkin, B. A., *A Treasury of American Anecdotes* (New York: Random House, 1957), pp. 47-48.

Brookes, Stella Brewer, *Joel Chandler Harris—Folklorist* (Athens: The University of Georgia Press, 1950).

Fuermann, George, *Reluctant Empire* (New York: Doubleday, 1957).

Hollon, W. Eugene, *The Southwest: Old and New* (New York: Alfred A. Knopf Co., 1961).

Hughes, Langston, *The Books of Negro Humor* (New York: Dodd, Mead, and Co., 1966), pp. 47-52.

ARTICLES

Dorson, Richard M., "The Negro," *American Folklore* (Chicago: University of Chicago Press, 1959), pp. 166-98.

Griffin, William J., "Review of Dog Ghosts," *Tennessee Folklore Society Bulletin*, XXIV (December, 1958), 157.

UNPUBLISHED MATERIALS

Byrd, James W., Interview with J. Mason Brewer, Salisbury, N. C., December 22, 1966.

Russell, Robert L., Taped Interview with J. Mason Brewer, University of North Carolina, Chapel Hill, March 12, 1967.

Turner, Kenneth W., "Negro Collectors of Negro Folklore: A Study of J. Mason Brewer and Zora Neale Hurston." Unpublished Master's Thesis, East Texas State University, Commerce, Texas, 1964.